HUMAN BODY ANIMAL BODIES

MUSCLES AND MOVEMENT

Izzi Howell

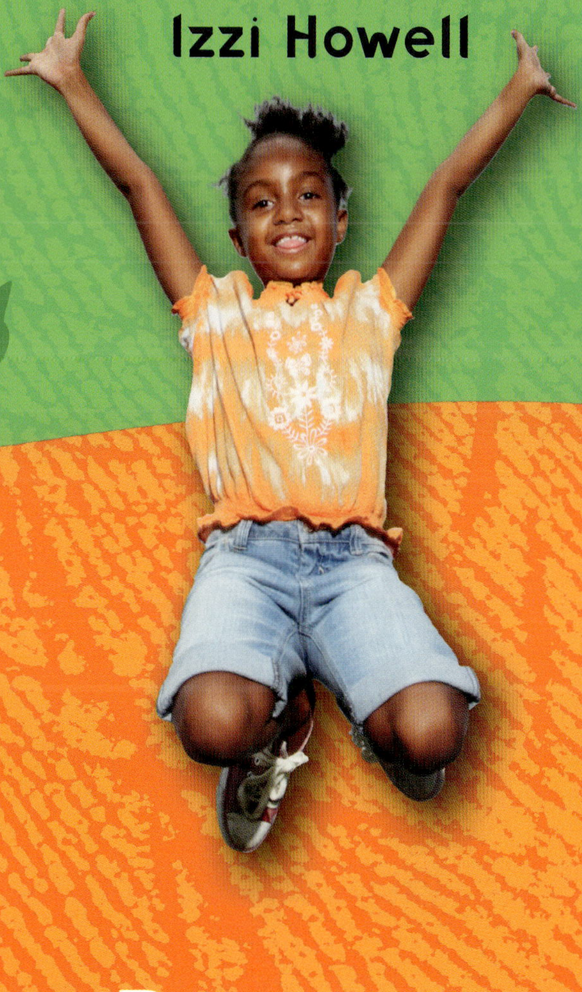

PowerKiDS press

Published in 2024 by The Rosen Publishing Group, Inc.
2544 Clinton Street, Buffalo, NY 14224

First published in Great Britain in 2017 by Wayland

Picture credits:
Getty: GlobalStock title page and 15, luamduan 5bl, Delpixart 8tl, GlobalP 9t, USO 11c, FatCamera 12, mauribo 13, spxChrome 14t, Freder 14bl, zefart 18–19b, OceanBodhi 20; Shutterstock: Arlene Gapusan cover t, Valentyna Chukhlyebova cover b, Potapov Alexander 4l, Aila Images 4r, Potapov Alexander 5t, Suphatthra China 5br, Skalapendra 6, holbox 7t, xpixel 7c, hsagencia 7b, ninii 8tr, Marco Tomasini 8b, Eric Isselee 9bl and 17c, givaga 9br, javarman 10l, VaLiza 10r, BORINA OLGA 11t, RusticBoy 11b, Johan Swanepoel 13, Svetlana Foote 13, pirita 13, ArtFamily 13, Richard Peterson 13, Vladimir Melnik 14br, EpicStockMedia 16, Rich Carey 17t, Vangert 17b, Kirsanov Valeriy Vladimirovich 18t, Nejron Photo 19tl, Ambient Ideas 19tr, RamonaS 21t, RamonaS 21b.

Editor: Izzi Howell
Design: Clare Nicholas

The author, Izzi Howell, is a writer and editor specializing in children's educational publishing.

Cataloging-in-Publication Data
Names: Howell, Izzi.
Title: Muscles and movement / Izzi Howell.
Description: New York : Powerkids Press, 2024. | Series: Human body, animal bodies | Includes index.
Identifiers: ISBN 9781642828153 (pbk) | ISBN 9781642828160 (library bound) | ISBN 9781642828177 (ebook)
Subjects: LCSH: Animal mechanics--Juvenile literature | Body mechanics--human-- Juvenile literature | Muscles-- Juvenile literature | Skeleton--Juvenile literature
Classification: LCC OL806.5 H69 2024 | DDC 573.7--dc23

Manufactured in the United States of America

CPSIA Compliance Information: Batch #CSPK24. For further information contact Rosen Publishing at 1-800-237-9932.

Contents

Skeleton

Inside a human body, there is a skeleton made of bones joined together.

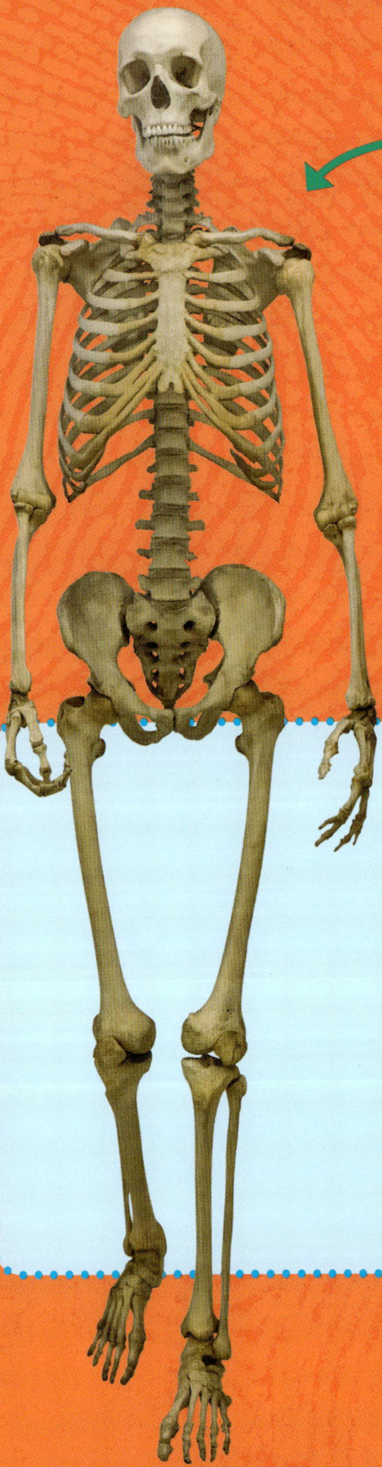

There are 206 bones in an adult skeleton.

Our skeleton helps us move. It also protects the inside of our body.

protect: to keep safe

Many animals also have a skeleton.

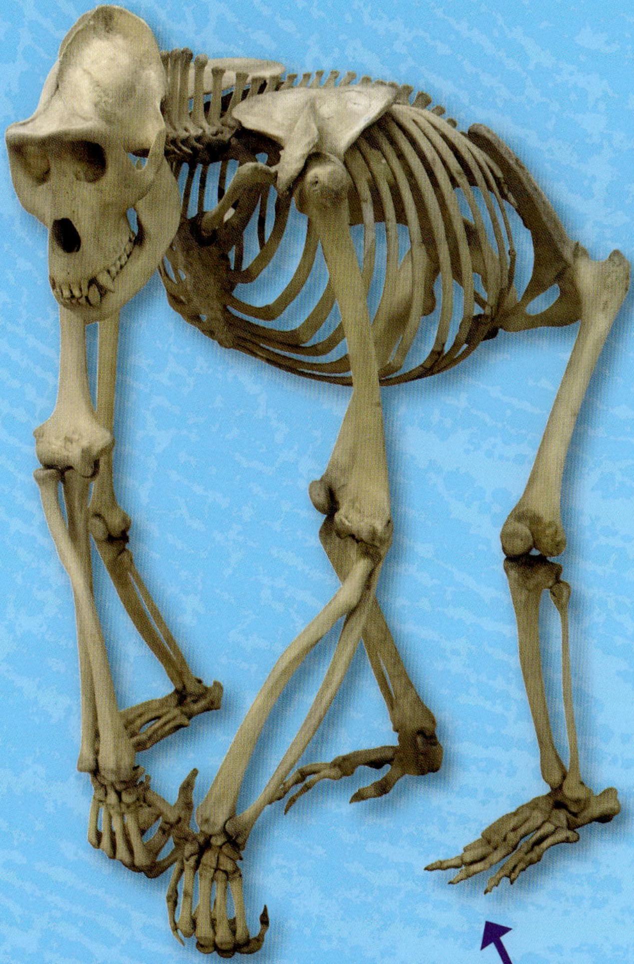

Squawk!

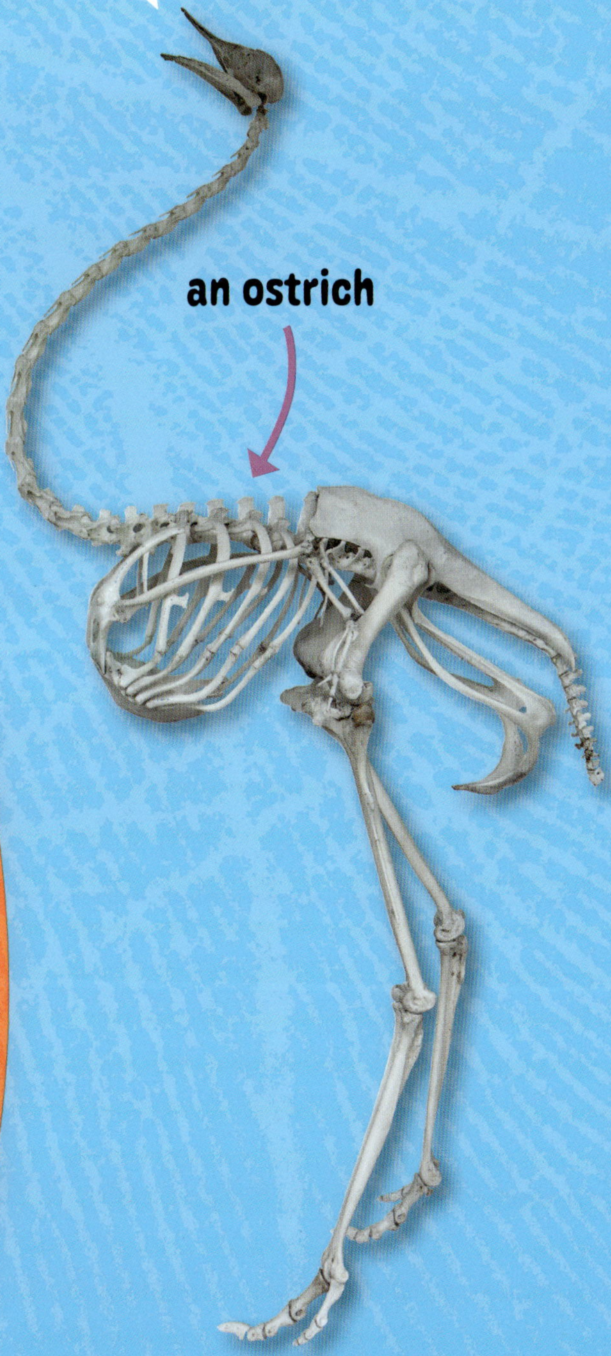

an ostrich

a gorilla

Which animal does this skeleton come from?

Muscles

Humans and most animals have muscles inside their body. Muscles pull on our bones to help us move.

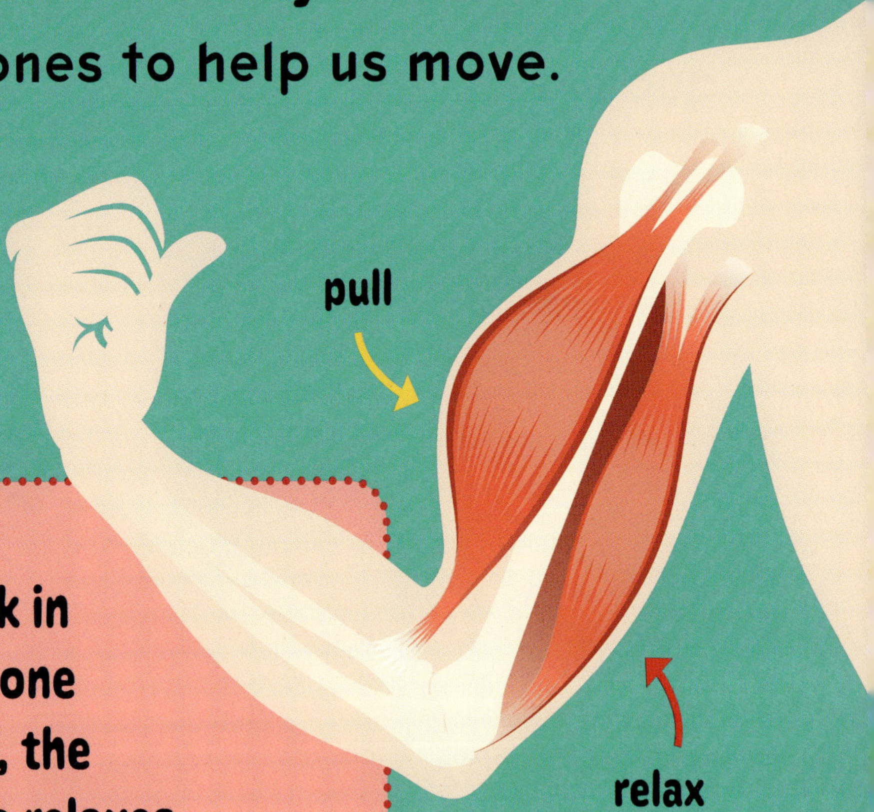

Muscles work in pairs. When one muscle pulls, the other muscle relaxes.

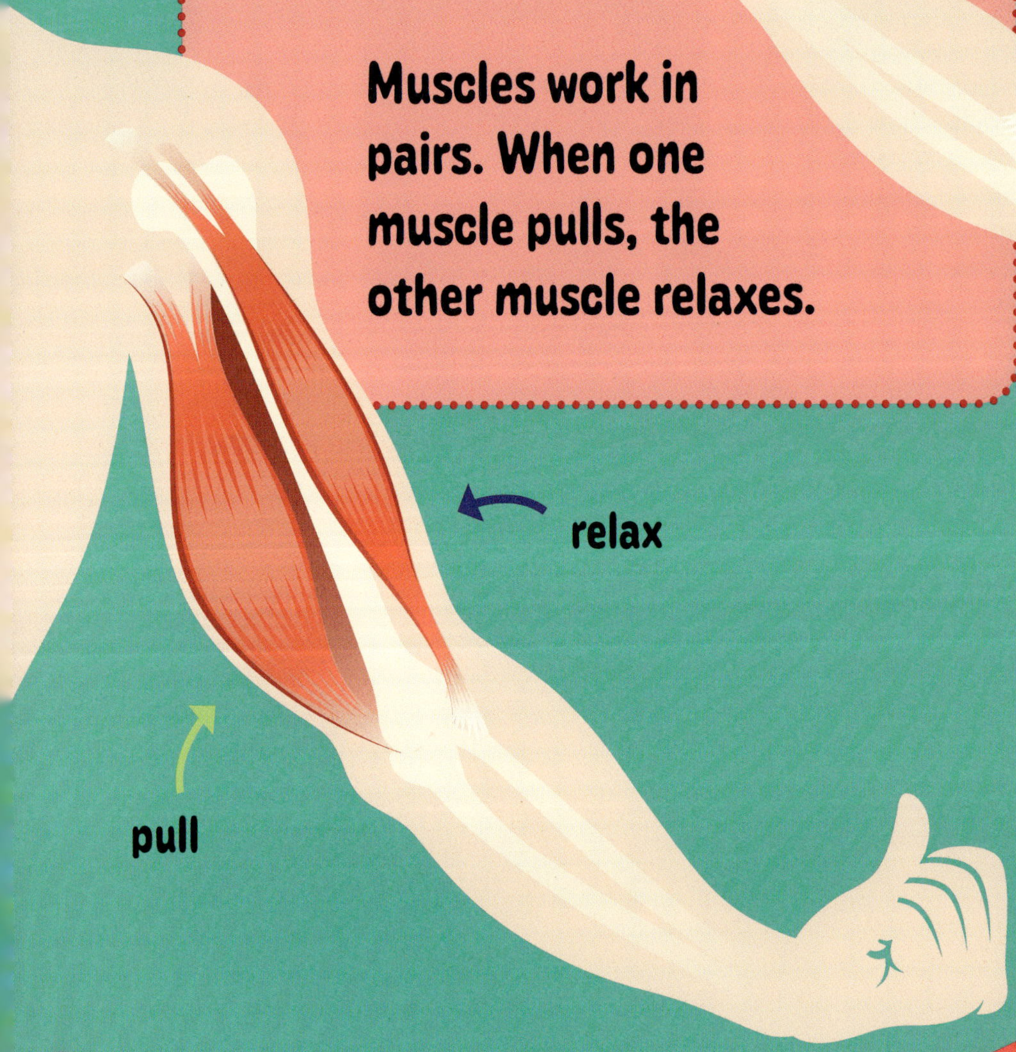

Some animals don't have skeletons, but they do have muscles. They use their muscles to move their body.

a jellyfish

a snail

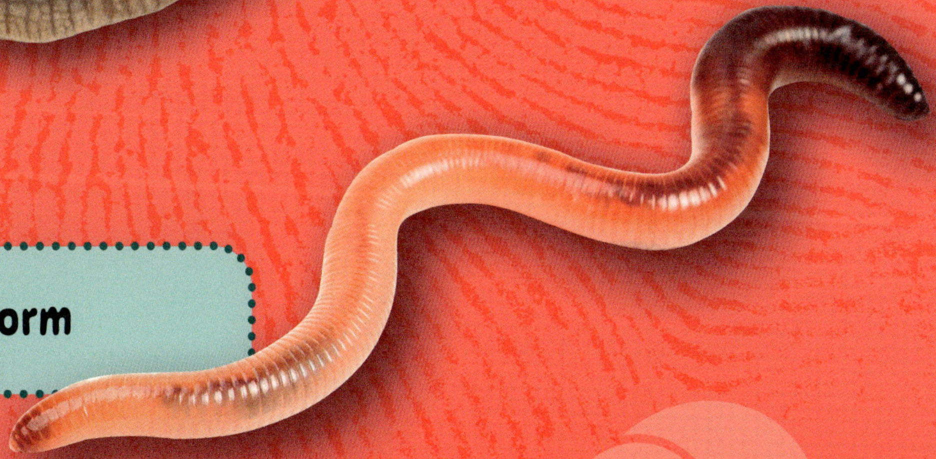

an earthworm

Exoskeletons

Animals without a skeleton protect their body in other ways. Some animals have a hard covering on the outside of their body called an exoskeleton.

a crab

a ladybug

a clam

Which animal on page 7 has an exoskeleton?

Some animals need a bigger exoskeleton as they grow larger.

The praying mantis sheds its smaller exoskeleton. Then it grows a bigger exoskeleton.

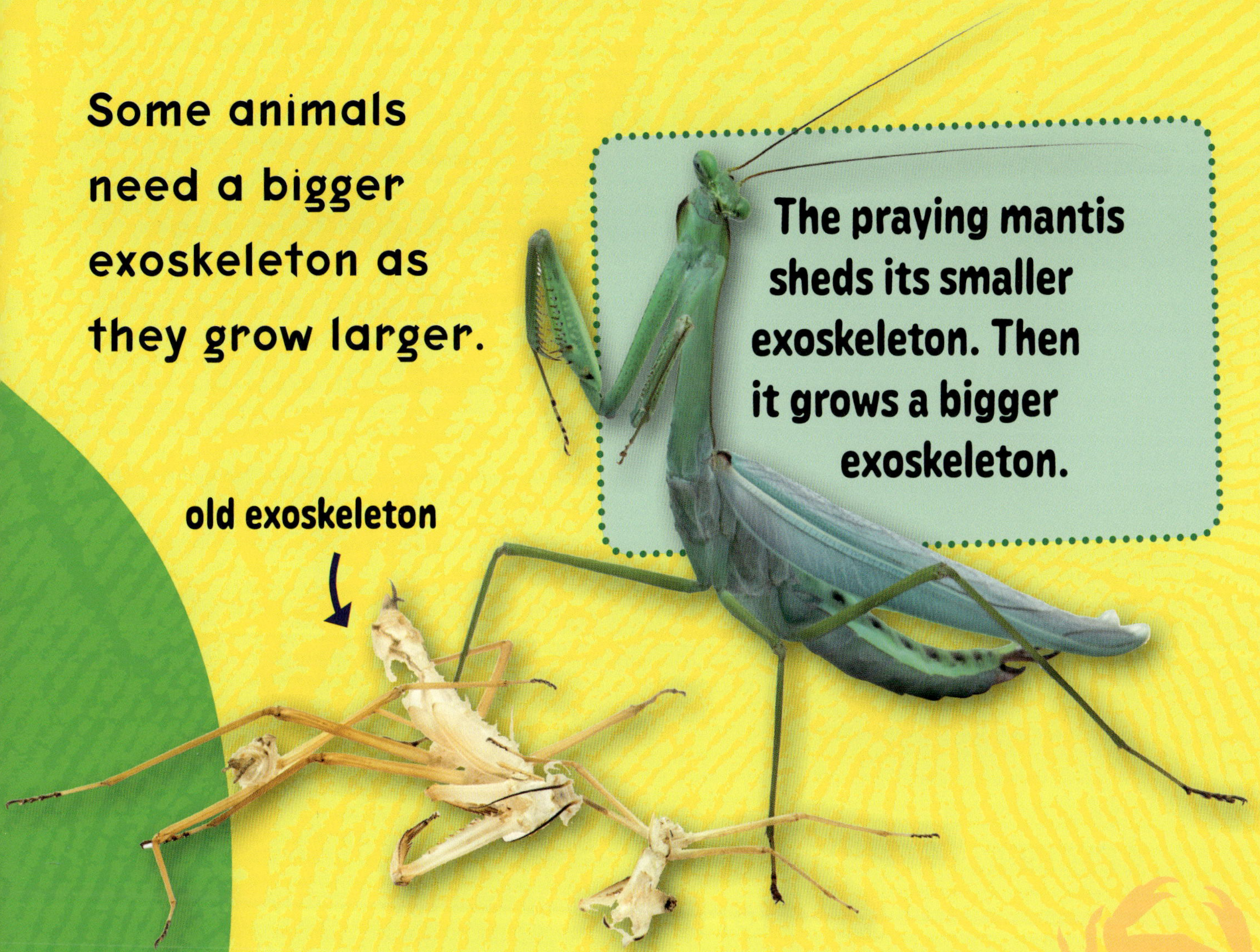

The hermit crab uses a shell from another animal as its exoskeleton. It finds a new, larger shell when it gets bigger.

shed: to lose skin or hair because it falls off

Walking

Humans and some animals walk on two legs. One foot stays on the ground while the other foot lifts up and moves forward.

Many animals walk on four or more legs.

Which animal moves on eight legs?

Running

Running is faster than walking. When we run, we bend our knees and push harder against the ground with our feet.

Sometimes, both our feet come off the ground.

Some animals can run much faster than humans.

a cheetah

a springbok

a hare

a horse

a human

an elephant

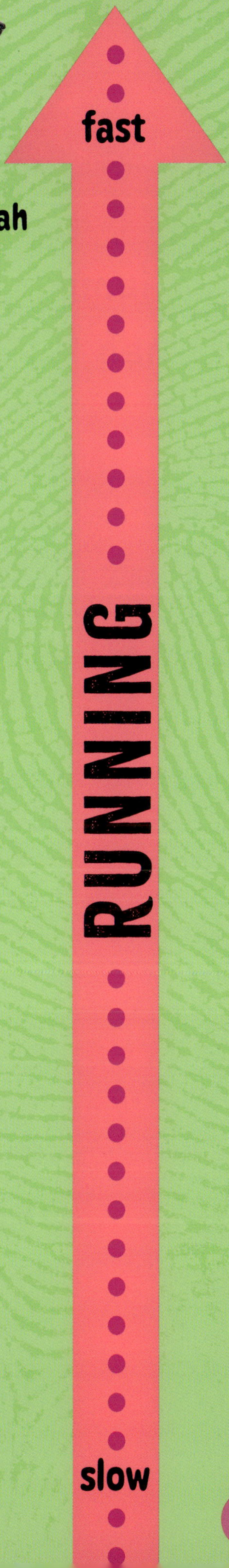

Jumping

To jump, humans and animals bend their knees. Then they push themselves up off the ground.

Humans and animals jump for many reasons.

a kangaroo

to move around

to get from one place to another

a polar bear

for fun!

a human

Swimming

Some animals that live in water swim to move around. Humans can also learn to swim.

Animals use different parts of their body to swim.

a sea turtle

front flippers

a frog

back legs

a goldfish

whole body and tail

Which body parts do humans use to swim?

Flying

Some animals can fly.

Flying animals have wings.

a bat

Animals fly by flapping their wings up and down. This pushes them through the air.

a parrot
a butterfly
a seagull

Special movement

Some animals move in special ways!

An octopus sucks in water and then shoots it out of its body to push itself forward.

Snakes do not have any arms or legs. They use their muscles to move their body from side to side. This pushes them forward.

Mudskippers are fish that can live on land or in water. In water, they use their fins to swim. On land, they walk on their fins!

Human and animal movement

Mammals

bat
cheetah
dog
elephant
gorilla
hare
horse
human
kangaroo
polar bear
springbok

FEATURES

skeleton, usually move on four legs, but not always

Birds

ostrich
parrot
penguin
seagull

FEATURES

skeleton, walk on two legs

Fish

goldfish
mudskipper

FEATURES

skeleton, swim

Amphibians

frog

FEATURES

skeleton, usually move on four legs

Minibeasts

ant

butterfly

earthworm

ladybug

praying mantis

snail

FEATURES

no skeleton, sometimes have an exoskeleton

Invertebrates

clam

crab

hermit crab

jellyfish

octopus

FEATURES

no skeleton, sometimes have an exoskeleton

Reptiles

Komodo dragon

sea turtle

snake

FEATURES

skeleton, usually move on four legs, but not always

Index

Answers

page 5 – A fish
page 8 – A snail
page 11 – A spider
page 17 – Arms and legs